Contents

James and Gran	2
Gran's sisters	3
Gran's Grandma	4
Gran's oldest photo	5
James and his bike	6
Go-carts	7
Football	8
Dolls and books	9
Comics	10
Punch and Judy	11
James at school	12
Gran at school	13
At the seaside	14
Happy Birthday, Gran	16

James and Gran

James likes this photo of Gran's birthday party best of all.

James likes to see what he was like when he was little.

Gran's sisters

Molly Lucy Jean Elsie Nan

This is Gran with her sisters at her 65th birthday party last year.
They are all Grandmas now.

Elsie Lucy Cousin Ted Jean

Molly

"Nan" when she was little

c. 1930

This is an older photo. How can you tell?

It is of Gran with her sisters and their cousin Ted when they were children.

Gran's Grandma

1923

Gran has kept an old photo of herself when she was a baby.

She is with her mother and her grandmother.

Gran's oldest photo

c. 1900

This is the oldest photo in Gran's album. It's very old, much older than Gran. It's Gran's Grandma at a wedding.

No one in this picture is alive today, so Gran's not quite sure who all the people are.

Have you ever seen an old photo like this?

James and his bike

Gran likes this photo of James on his new bike.

Both Gran and Grandad remember playing when they were little, many years ago.

Home-made land yacht, 1955

Go-carts

Gran and Grandad remember making go-carts like this when they were young.

They didn't have a bicycle to ride.

What games did your grandparents play when they were young?

Football

c.1935

Grandad

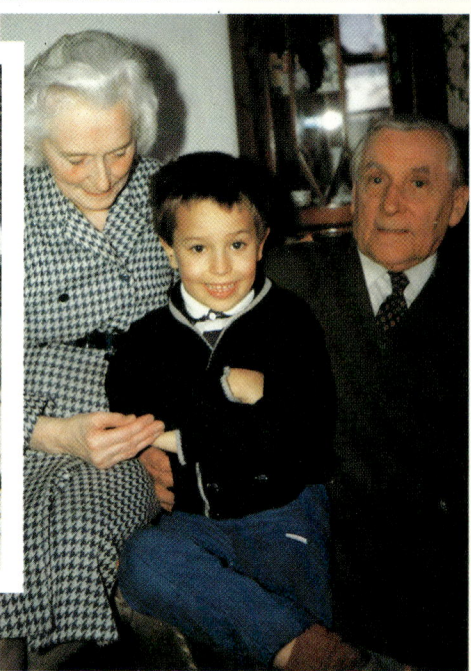

James's Grandad used to play football in the school team.

Grandad goes to watch football today.

James also likes playing football.

What do you like playing?

8

Dolls and books

'Florence' doll, 1914

James likes to ask Gran questions.

"What toys did you have when you were little?"

Gran says, "Once I had a doll like this. She had a china face and I broke it.

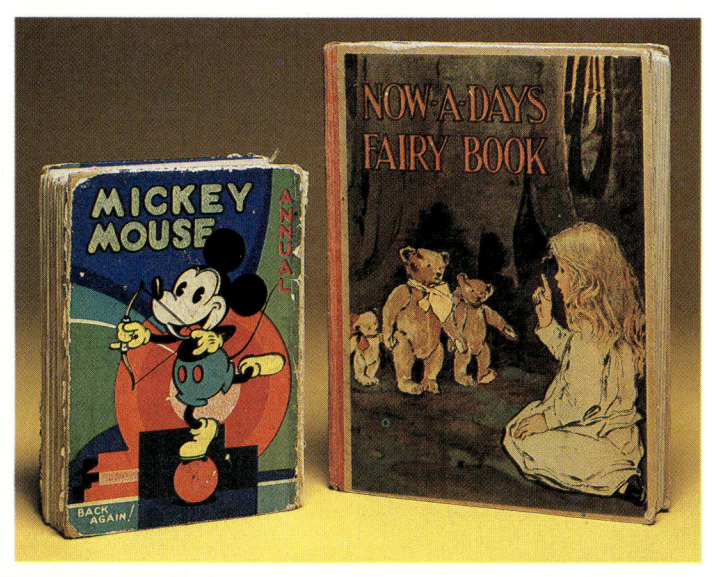

But I have kept these old books which my Mum and Dad gave me when I was a little girl."

Comics

James likes to read.

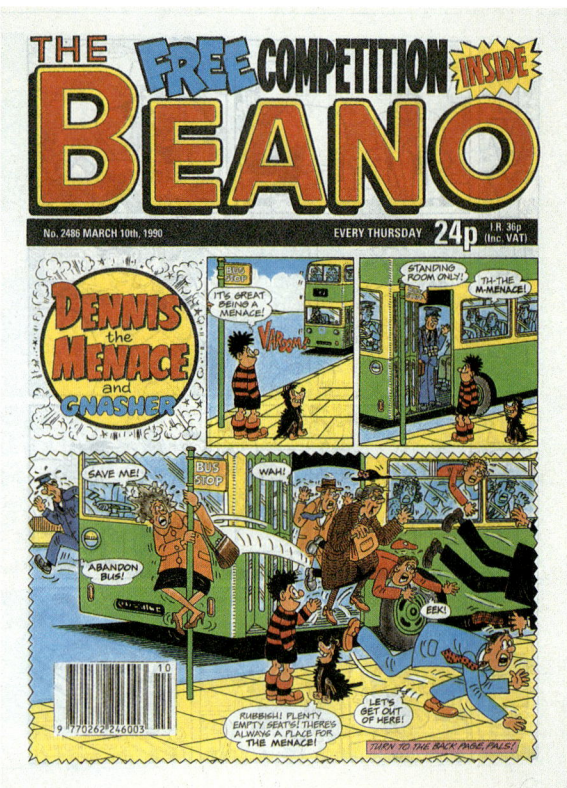

His Gran bought him a Beano comic.

Gran remembers reading the very first Beano comic over fifty years ago.
This is what it looked like.

Is it the same today?

Punch and Judy

Punch and Judy show, Ilfracombe, 1894

Gran told James, "Long ago, when my Mum was a little girl, there were no comics to read. But she liked to watch the Punch and Judy show."

What do you watch at home?

James at school

Last year, James went to a Christmas party at his school.

Can you find him in this photo?

Tarvin Primary School, Cheshire, 1988

Did you go to a Christmas party last year?

Gran at school

St. Jude's School, Wolverhamton, c. 1927

Gran has kept this old photo of her classroom.
It is nearly sixty years old.

What can you see?

How old is your school?
Are there any old photos of your school?

At the seaside

BUDLEIGH SALTERTON   MARINE PARADE   C 4366

Each summer, Gran likes to go to the seaside for a holiday.
She always goes to the same place.

Last year she sent James this postcard.

Gran's Grandma used to go to the same place too.

Budleigh Salterton, c. 1860

She gave Gran this very old postcard.

Look at the postcards. Are they the same? What is new?

James can see how the place has changed.

Some people collect old postcards. They can tell us a lot about places in the past.

Happy Birthday, Gran

Many things have changed since Gran was little.
But some have stayed the same.

Can you find out about some of them?

HAPPY BIRTHDAY, GRAN!